The Sleeping Beauty

Easy piano picture book

Music by Pyotr Ilyich Tchaikovsky
arranged by Alan Gout
Text by Catherine Storr
Illustrations by Julek Heller

Faber & Faber
in association with Faber Music Ltd

Other Easy Piano Picture Books:

THE SNOWMAN
Words and music by Howard Blake
Illustrated by Dianne Jackson

SWAN LAKE
Words by Catherine Storr
Music by Tchaikovsky
Illustrated by Dianne Jackson

HANSEL AND GRETEL
Words by Catherine Storr
Music by Humperdinck
Illustrated by Annabel Spenceley

THE NUTCRACKER
Words by Catherine Storr
Music by Tchaikovsky
Illustrated by Dianne Jackson

THE MIKADO
Words by Kenneth Lillington
Music by Sullivan
Illustrated by Jenny Tylden-Wright

A CHRISTMAS CAROL
Words by Kenneth Lillington
Eight traditional Christmas songs
Illustrated by Annabel Spenceley

CATS
Based on 'Old Possum's Book of
Practical Cats' by T.S. Eliot
Music by Andrew Lloyd Webber
Illustrated by Ann Aldred

The Sleeping Beauty

In the palace of King Florestan and his Queen,
great preparations were being made for the
christening of their baby daughter, Aurora.
The old master of ceremonies, Catalabetto,
welcomed the guests and the six fairies who had
been invited to be the godmothers of the little
princess. Last and most important of these
was the Lilac Fairy.

Andantino

The fairies went up to the baby's cradle and gave her gifts
of beauty, wisdom and grace; but just before the Lilac Fairy
could speak, a tremendous noise at the door announced
the arrival of the wicked fairy, Carabosse, who
by mistake had not been invited to the ceremony.

In her fury, she pulled out the hair
of Catalabetto, who had left her name
off the list of invited guests. Then,
approaching the cradle, she
announced that one day Aurora
would prick her finger and that
this would bring about her death.

Horror-stricken, the King and Queen implored Carabosse to forgive them and to take back the curse, but she only gloated in her evil. The whole court was in despair. But the Lilac Fairy, who had hidden herself when Carabosse entered, now stepped forward and said: "The little princess shall not die when she pricks her finger. She will fall into a deep sleep, which will last until a Prince is brave enough to seek her out and waken her with a kiss."

Time passed. Aurora grew up into a lovely, charming girl, and preparations were made to celebrate her sixteenth birthday. Catalabetto came out of the palace, and saw a group of girls dancing as they sewed with needles, which the King had banished from the country in order to try to save Aurora from the wicked fairy's curse. The King ordered that they should be punished, but then he relented. "No one shall be unhappy on the princess's birthday," he said.

Four young princes now appeared to ask for
Aurora's hand in marriage. They watched her
dance, and she danced with each in turn,
but she did not want to make up her mind
to marry any one of them.

Then she noticed an old woman holding a spindle, something she had never seen. She asked to look at it, then danced with it in her hand, but suddenly – she pricked her finger. Terrified, she implored help from her frightened parents, but then fell unconscious into a death-like sleep. The old woman then revealed herself as the wicked fairy, Carabosse, exulting in the curse she had laid on Aurora sixteen years ago.

As the whole court mourned, the Lilac Fairy
appeared. "Do not grieve. I will lay upon you all
an enchanted sleep, so that a hundred years may pass
without your knowing. When Aurora wakes to the
Prince's kiss, you will wake too, and your lives will
go on from where they now leave off," she said.
As she spoke, the King and Queen, the nobles, the
courtiers, the pages, ladies-in-waiting, the maids,
the cooks, even the scullions in the King's
kitchen, all fell asleep where they stood.

The Lilac Fairy left the palace. Dust began to settle on the rooms, spiders wove cobwebs round the tables and chairs, and in the garden roses ran wild and grew into a thick hedge of thorns round the sleeping palace.

Nearly a hundred years later, the young Prince
Florimund was hunting in the woods by a river.
He and his friends stopped to have a meal,
and to dance on the smooth green turf.

When the rest of the party went off to resume hunting,
the prince was tired and chose to remain alone by
the river. The Lilac Fairy appeared, and showed
him a vision of the Princess Aurora, asleep in
the sleeping palace.

Florimund immediately saw that she was
the loveliest princess in the world,
and fell deeply in love with her.

The Lilac Fairy brought the dream Aurora to dance
with the prince, who implored the Fairy, "Where
is this beautiful girl? Take me to her, so that I may
marry her and make her my Queen."

The Lilac Fairy led the prince to the gates of the
sleeping palace. There Carabosse kept guard, so
that her evil spell should continue to hold Aurora.
But Florimund, helped by the Lilac Fairy, overcame
Carabosse and cut his way through the wilderness
of thorns till he reached the centre of the palace.

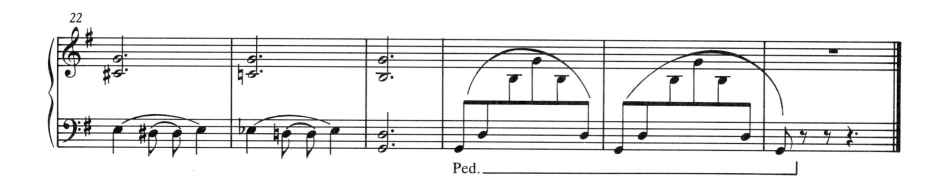

There he found Aurora, deeply
asleep on her couch, surrounded
by the sleeping courtiers. She was
even more beautiful than the girl he
had seen in the dream, and he leaned
over her and kissed her on the lips.

Immediately, she opened her eyes and stirred,
and at the same moment all the people around her
woke too. The dust disappeared, the cobwebs vanished,
and everyone took up their lives as if they had been
asleep for no more than a minute, instead of a hundred years.

The wedding of Aurora and Florimund was a splendid
affair. The courtiers danced, the fairies danced, and
there were entertainments by fairy-tale characters:
the White Cat danced with Puss in Boots,
Red Riding Hood danced with the Wolf,
and the Blue Bird danced with the Enchanted Princess.

Allegro moderato e brillante

Aurora danced with Florimund and everyone
rejoiced that now the young couple might
live happily ever after.

CODA